in the
shade

dayna gosselin

*to my
inspiration*

trigger warning

the content beyond this page may contain triggering
and/or sensitive material

topics such as
addiction
trauma
mental health
and abuse
are explored

please seek assistance if needed

contents

in the
bottle

she rubs the bottle as if it's magic
like there's a genie at the bottom
waiting to hear her life's wishes
that she washes away
with each gulp

-wasted

your voice
calls my name
not to go past my
knees in water
but your fear
of drowning
not waves
pulls me deep
under

-hand me downs

pot without a lid
boiling over
overflowing onto
everything
it's my anger
sometimes the heat
turns down
just to let me simmer
though my dial
easily alters
from summer
to winter

-changing seasons

sometimes she wonders
who the better
liar is
you
or the mirror
when you say
she is beautiful

you fed me compliments
but i was never full

she fell in love
maybe one night
it will be with
herself

i crave to travel
from my skin
to cradle the edges
of someone else's
bones
i want to inhabit
their being
to wear the perfect
curves
men desire to
explore
i crave to be
anyone
other than me
because maybe then
i'll be

happy

i coloured
in the lines
for so long
that when my hand
fell over the edges
creating a butterfly
i desperately begged
for the caterpillar

she couldn't separate him from the sin
she believed he declared war
when he was already battling himself

-internal battle

it feels like
drowning
in shallow water
swallowing
wave after wave
finding
yourself six feet under
until
you can't be saved

when i die
pour my ashes
into a river
so i can finally be
at peace
while drowning

you acted as if my red words meant it was okay for
you to go through
ignoring the signal to slow down
to stop
weren't you taught
by your mother
how to drive
or your father
if only you listened
i wouldn't be here now wishing
or asking myself
why
to the world
to the man
that made me feel so empty
like the street i go by
every day in the morning
as a passenger
where the only traffic is in my head
trying to understand how no meant yes

-no means no

hidden in my mind
i promised
never to search for you
but you always find me
then beg me
to visit

-trauma

laying on clouds
of pillows
with a clouded mind
ingesting pills to float
away from my bed
where my pain
is out of sight
i've counted so many times
but my head still isn't filled
with sheep
go away
i demand
but memories
can be so mean

body survived
but not alive
on the inside
just a disguise
i can't describe
until you've died
too

he was taught
if he wasn't the perpetrator
he'd be the victim

but the judge sentenced him anyway

he bottled his emotions
then drank it

-empty again

i am in pieces
scattered from lessons
and values
mixed with aggression

i am broken
into sections that
someone reads
poking fun
at my imperfections

i am the bestseller

i say i am good
as everyone takes
their look

but one thing i am not
is the front
of my book

-the cover

we spread lies
like a game
of hot potato
passing it on as quickly
as possible
to keep the heat
off us

she's continuously blinded
by light and darkness
that she can't envision
in between
her black and white thinking
rigid ways
made everything
all bad
all good
forgetting that a sheep
can act like a wolf
when put in the wrong
cage

i can't understand
why we say
always and never
when these absolutes
are not absolutely
the truth

-all or nothing

you say you want to
go to college
buy a house
get married
have children

didn't they tell you
that life doesn't always follow your plans
i wanted to be happy

you see it happening
but i'm blind
with perfect eyes
not able to envision a future
with these
broken glasses
of mine

-cracked lens

you say it's in my head
that's partly true
because my head is congested
with thoughts of death
from this emotional flu

my body can't function
or play sports with my son
he's asked me why
so many times
so now he only begs for
his mom

she doesn't think i try
but i know that i'm trying
i feel buried alone
in our relationship
she says is dying

told my doctor something's wrong
he said i'm right
gave me these pills
said to go home
now everything's all right

but it wasn't

so i wrote them a note
on a shady day

to tell them daddy left
hoping their fog
would eventually fade

it read

i'll now be the angel to whom you pray

out of
the bottle

you're not lost
you've just found yourself
on an adventure

regardless of what people say
talk is not cheap
words cost people their happiness
and some spend years
trying to recover

-be kind always

take the weight off my shoulders
let me unload my troubles
for they are too heavy
to carry alone
because i know
i can
become stable again
with your unconditional
support

-helping hands

do not tell a storm to relax
i need to pour
i need to scream
until i see
the sun come back
again

-brighter days ahead

don't say get over it when they're trying to just get
through it

-advice to the reader

you're the only one
who can save yourself
from the demons within
they cannot fight your battle
but they can teach you
how to use your
weapon

-friends and family and counselors

you do not need to walk in their shoes
to know they are tired
you just need to remind them
how far they have come

-empathy

practice makes perfect
resilient individuals

-keep going

i want the ability to reason with others
even when
i'm angry
i want to make rational decisions
even when
i'm emotional
but most of all
i need the ability to seek help
even when
i don't want to

-work in progress

thank your body
for the home
that moves
wherever you go
make repairs
when it's run down
and it's okay
to ask for help
instead of tearing it
to the ground

-renovations

facing you
never made me smile
until i put the past
behind me
finally standing
in front of a mirror
once again

-reflecting

to those with anxiety

realize if you're going to die you will die whether
you pursue your dreams or not
realize that suffocating in public while pursing your
dreams is better than suffocating in your bed
realize that avoidance only makes things harder
realize that this darkness can be overcome by facing
your worst fears
realize that this is not the end
realize that this is just the beginning
realize that you will find your greatest strengths in
times of weakness
realize that you will not allow this to control or
dictate your life
realize that you have so much life in you
realize caffeine is not your friend
realize that this
is your sign

sincerely

someone overcoming anxiety

he flirted with death
until he found love
of life

-now he's committed

give yourself
what you always
wanted

unconditional love

it's not right to say
you'll give them a taste of their own
medicine

why inject them with pain
when that's all they've ever
felt

inject them with kindness

i've watched sinners
turn to saints
trying to resurrect
what good is underneath
uncovering the dirt
from where they were

buried alive

how lucky we are
to feel pain
because experiences
are hidden lessons
teaching us
from loss
comes gain

they did not take your voice
you were developing it

-be loud be clear

society labeled me a victim
and i refuse to carry that name
tag on my body
because i never thought of myself
as anything other than
an experienced advocate

-reframe

there is a beauty
and beast within her
i love both
unconditionally

-wildly beautiful

i may not see the shadow that follows you
hear the voices that speak to you
or understand how aliens abducted you
but it doesn't make it less real
than me
because i know
it's real to you

-define reality

time cannot heal those who keep reopening their
wounds

-my experience

if you are bitter
with an aftertaste
from your past
focus on the sweetness
in your present
let it fade the sorrow
off your tongue
as your feed your soul
with forgiveness

-you are strong

there's enough darkness in the world
when the day ends
empower and inspire light
to help our friends carry on
during their darkest
nights

-teach them

you're addicted to one feeling
that hinders
your ability
to feel hundreds of wonderful things
in the world

there's more to feel than pain

never forget
you are art
regardless of the critics

-beautiful

there is a world war
enlisting our support
an internal battle
in every person
we need to fight
together

-allies

if only we could judge a book
by its cover
to know when
someone needs
our help

we say to our children
it's okay
don't cry
we think it's okay to tell them what to feel
we think it's okay to tell them how to react
maybe they are not okay
maybe we need to say
it's okay to cry
because how can we expect the same children
to reach out
when they need help
to the ones who speak for them
to the ones who never validated their emotions

it's okay if we change our language

mental health is a never ending battle
you may fight with your family and friends
but never forget
they are your
armour

-supports

no
say it
practice it
learn it
use it
teach it
accept it
that's it

-to my future children

if you don't believe in magic
you've never watched
a frown disappear
and turn into

a smile

be the candle in someone's power outage
it might be the only way
they can see ahead

tried to put myself in someone else's shoes
but for some reason
it never fit
i could never walk a day in their life
but i could see their shoes
wear away
in different places

so i reminded them to take a break
like my father taught me
and i asked them
about the different types of tears
they experienced
what worked best for them
to keep on walking

and
i promised myself
to never forget
to ask
how they were doing
because i too
know what it's like
to be tired

-carrying on

in the

covers

our currency of love
just made me feel broke
with an exchange rate
so high

-bankrupt

you were a blank canvas
he decided to use
painting a picture
of distorted love
with his wet paintbrush

-he called you his masterpiece

if only it were a piece of cake
he craved
instead of a piece of me

i am not whole anymore

we were children
but somehow you knew
what adults did

or maybe it
was just what your father
did

do not make a promise
you cannot keep
like the time you said
you would protect
your own

but forgot your shield
when you left them alone
with him

i like how
my thoughts are completely mine
untouchable
even when
my body isn't

she took everything with a grain of sugar
until you fed her salt

-no longer sweet and innocent

pulling at my heartstrings
creating a scene
in front of an audience
i'm too embarrassed
red faced from your script
i'm improvising to avoid critics
acting happy
pretending i love your character
until the curtains close
and the show is over

behind the scenes is worse

finally built immunity
to your virus
after years of pain

-numb

the last time my mother held me
was in her stomach
stretched wide for my embrace
but nine months of providing warmth
must have been enough for
her

maybe that's why
i'm so cold

i was not blinded by love
my eyes adjusted to your darkness
where i began to see pain
as normal

my paper thin skin
tore from pages of words
you called me

filed into my mind
beside
a shredder
that's
b r o k e n

this page
is as empty
as you made me
feel

i once wore my heart on my sleeve
but i was stripped
down

i was in pieces
and you carefully removed me
from the instability
to place me on top
of the world

only to knock me down
again

like i was a game
of jenga
and this was your strategy
to keep me from
winning

-unstable structure

why do i want to run back
to what i ran from
why do i crave hell
when it took me so long
to reach haven

we had a spark
the kind that ignited a flame
for our demons to play
together
the kind that swallowed
any angel left on our shoulder
the older
we became
the kind that burned us
out
from heated
conversation
and justified temptation
the kind i never want
to come about

ever again

you said
i was digging myself a hole
but i saw you
building a fortress
maybe all i was trying to do
was find another way
in

but you still found a way to keep me out

you burned the bridge we built
my only connection
from this lonely place
so i swore i'd find my way
back to your side
even if it meant
swimming over bodies of water
and drowning
because without you
i don't know how
to survive

you're either taught
to be the giver
or the taker

-life

you're holding on
to a rope
slipping away
from your grasp
burning your hands
peeling every inch
of your self worth
with blood
sweat and tears falling below
where you once stood
and somehow
you're still hanging in there
because he begged
don't let me go

yet his hands are unscathed

the wilting rose petals
beneath my fingertips
do not decide if
you love me
or not

you do

i wanted you to love me
so i gave up loving myself
to make room

i raised you up
placing you on a pedestal
then begged

don't look down on me

-irony

because i gave everything to him
i became nothing
to me

-giving up

she gave him a home in her heart
but all he wanted was to relocate

you were my safety net
catching me when i fell
i guess it was too often
because you wore away
to become nothing
at all

-torn

built a wall from my
broken pieces and your
broken promises
it was only right to
fit them together

-barrier

love cannot be fractioned

you do

_____

or you do not

you kissed my wounds
then reopened them when you were mad
you pretended to be an angel
but your lips gave
the kiss of
death

the problem was
i spent my life
buying love
with my self worth

-broke/n

you see a lover
i see a liar

–split vision

i did not welcome the truth
i did not have a sign under my nose
inviting it in
but that did not matter
because the truth is
an expected guest
and i still haven't decided
if you get to stay

-wisdom

you worry
that your secrets aren't as safe
as i made them seem
behind my lips and behind our walls
as much as i want to spill the hurt
you caused me
onto paper
i don't want to make a mess
when i've practiced so hard
to be clean
just like you wanted

-about you

confined to a frame called picture perfect

that's all it ever was

how can i find my way back to you
if we forgot to build the road

-roadblock

your blinker signaled me
not to get in
but your voice
welcomed me to sit
i'd been a passenger
for far too long
i had forgotten how to drive
so i let you steer me
down the back road
to a place i swore to never visit
passing the crash site
we barely survived
continuing right through
memory lane

out of
the covers

if you're reading this
you're alive
you still have time
to heal

they said the pain was from heartbreak
but i knew they were wrong

it was from growing

sometimes closure means
never walking through
that open door
again

they were a kite
looking down on the ones
who held their string
who helped them to fly
you pushed them to be better
and they became high
from ego
but even the strongest winds
die down
sometimes they forget
and when they come crashing
into the ground
let the rocks be the first to welcome them
to level them out

-rock bottom

if they stab you in the back
take the knife out
then cut the hold they have on you
and never look back

do not let the ones
who hurt you
try to heal you

you either
build me up or
break me down
so i took away
your power
tools

-i'm in control

you've ignited
a flame within me
that no one could ever put out
a long lasting
fire burning
from your words of
doubt

there are
people who water your ideas
and people who cut them down
but do not be fooled
they both
allow you to grow

you were a gun
i was ammunition
and i
was the only one
who could load the power
you held over my head

-disarmed

and it was a relief to know
my heart was only
metaphorically in your hands
so when you dropped me
i did not fall
i did not break
i continued to beat
in my chest
where i belong

-strong hold

if they made you feel
unlovable
it's not about you
and never was
it is a reflection of
their self
and their fear
from an absence of love

but let it empower you
not hinder you
to love more
not less
because you know
what can happen
from love's absence

-stop the cycle

they did not kill you
they reminded you
of the warrior
within

-fighter

staring at you
next to me
so still in the frame
in a moment i no longer missed
who or where
i was
i knew for certain
i was
no longer still

when i finally realized we were going in circles
everything just seemed so straight

you can love again
just make sure
it's yourself first

i want the kind of love
that values
inner beauty

i hear it never ages
like us

i want someone to tear
the surface of my skin
and enter into my veins
swim with my sharks
and dance with my sun

all from deep
conversation

i learned
you do not fall in love
you fly in love

you cannot see
eye to eye
with someone
who thinks they're taller
than you

-big headed small minded

as we beat around the bush
we lose the seeds
from the back of our pockets
to plant our tree

-let us grow into a forest

i am not the piece to complete
your puzzle
i am a whole picture
you admire
in a museum of others
and if you picture yourself
hung next to me
for the rest of your life
you need to remember your place

you weren't the cure
when i was love sick
you were the vial
that held the medicine

and my god
i needed to be held
sometimes

you sheltered my insecurities
until i was ready to build a home
of acceptance within myself

the hurt i feel
spreads across your back
and you carry the pain
that weighs me down

your bones are strong
holding onto me
in the name of love
as mine break
in your arms

-my backbone

i was drowning
instead of pulling me out
you jumped in beside
teaching me how to swim
against the tide

-how to keep me afloat

your love
was a truth serum
for my soul

-therapy

gravity forces me
to remain on the ground
where my dreams
drift through the sky
out of reach
they speak
but you taught me
how to fly

-birds

to inspire
is the greatest gift
wrapped
carefully with love
a simple present
that only a few
know about

-thank you

through the years
i've travelled to many places
but my favourite place
remains
inside of your arms

it took me years to love myself
yet i loved you in one day

my home
isn't just a place
it's a feeling
i'll never sell
or dare to move
i've unpacked
my heart
and it's settled in
next to you

one day
i looked at you
knowing i loved you
not able to comprehend
how i didn't know
yesterday

-today

you're a star
so radiant
even in my darkest nights
your light
inspires mine
even when separated
by distance
i'll continue to
watch you
shine

you said seeing
is believing
so close your eyes
and tell me
if you can't see me
would you still know
i love you

tired hands from raising us
still you refuse
to ever put us down

-good parenting

your child is not a battleground
your child is a sign of peace
a treaty to never break

never walk away
from someone who chases you
through fire
to water your demons
and continues to stay
when it burns

-fire fighter

when they undress
the last secret from your body
for the first time
you'll know what it's like
to be completely naked

-exposed

i never had to give you a piece of myself
for you to be happy
it was refreshing feeling whole

your smile
extends from one cheek
to the other

then to mine

before you i ran from my demons
now we chase them together

-teammate

in the
light

my apology
to the ones
i've hated
for i used you
as an excuse
to not hate myself

my wounds are stitched
with every word
i write

-healing

i am happy
for the times
i have fallen
for it reminded me
to remain grounded

-sensible

i've chased happiness
across the world
running after people
trying to keep up with
societal standards and life expectations
the further i went
brought me closer to the secret
of winning
which was
i'm not competing
against anyone else
and there's no prize for racing
into things

-silver lining

i've been asked countless times
when i'm going to get married
and it's sad to think
a relationship without a legal title
is not worthy on its own
that this next step is expected
so i'm expected
to buy eyes
to celebrate my love
paying for recognition
of love i
only need to recognize
yet society plants the seed
by asking questions
that blossom in my mind
that without marriage
a relationship
cannot grow
i do
not want to water that idea
anymore

-black veil

people tell me
save for a house

but i'd rather
save for memories
that house my feelings
of home

if we all just became pleased
when people became pleased with their selves
happiness would not be
fractioned

-two birds one source

someone once said to me
focus on the now
now that
redefined my past
and changed my future
thank you for my present
it's the perfect
gift

i wish i was still in the moment
like i am in photographs

-moved

as a little girl
i painted a picture of the life
i wanted
not understanding at the time
events and people
will spill
all over it
creating the most beautiful
mess

-abstract

meeting someone new i ask
who are you
most say their name
few say their job
some say their age
and i began
to realize they were
defining their self
in the way
society does

so now i don't ask
who they are
instead i task myself
to find out
what makes you smile
and for me
it's always their answers

-defined

what's it like to find yourself
she asked him

he smiled
one minute you find yourself
and you blink because
it's natural
but when you open your eyes
you're gone
so you have to search
again

then what's the point
she wondered

he whispered
that one whole moment
will always be worth the game of
hide and seek

-personal growth

i wrote you a letter i'll never mail
i wrote you poems you'll never read
i wrote you songs you'll never hear

i wrote about you in everything

but when i finally spoke the words
it was obvious

i was writing to myself

i see more beauty
when closing my eyes
feeling every inch of
the world against my fingers
sounds vibrating my body
from leaves singing to the ground
smelling the music beneath
my feet standing tall
tasting clarity in the wind
with arms stretched wide
like tree branches
for the world's embrace
and i'm sensing
i can finally see

-breath of fresh air

inspiration can either come from
everything
or nothing
it either exists or it does not
there is no in between
but sometimes all you need
is a new lens
to finally see

-splitting

you are a consumer
taking values and views
from another
given to you
by our mother
an heirloom
passed down
each generation
if only the family tree
had less
saturation

-create your own path

she grew up believing
everything she was told
like how the tooth fairy
left money under her pillow
until she found her teeth
in a dresser drawer
imprisoned in a jar
just like her

-released

teary eyed she asked
what's the point of living

he wiped the tears away
with hands and words
my point in life is this

she then understood hers

the path to self awareness
leads you into a cave
uncovering the truth
under the surface of dirt
you need to
continuously
dig

every day

i watched my brother mislabel
sugar as salt
and it reminded me
it's human nature
to label with just
one look

-stop labeling people

i want you to recognize
my words
not my name
or my face

because maybe
my words
can bring change

to the world

i don't want to feel like my voice
has been heard
i want to know
indisputably
that it has been

my life changed when i turned cursing into cursive

-how the author was born

when their eyes light up
from gossip
begging for you to feed them wood
will you spark a new topic
or let innocent people burn

-two types of people

learn to swim with the sharks
before you get eaten

-jealousy

forget what you've been told
because sometimes
we need to
talk to a stranger
especially
when they're staring at you
in the mirror

-self reflection

i burned the city
populated by self destruction
to build a home
within the ashes

-growth

you lost sight of yourself
looking after other people
now it's time to see
who you find
searching for yourself

-search and rescue

when i was young
my father told me to invest
as early as possible

and now that i'm older
i now understand
so i began

to invest in myself

we lay you to rest
but it's too difficult to say
goodnight
because i know the darkest times
can come in
mourning

in the end
we're all just trying to arrive safely
at death's door
as an expected guest
with a painless invitation

i sat in the shade
waiting for the sun to hit me
as if light was expected
to just
follow darkness

i remained in the shade
for so long
i forgot
the feeling of the warm rays
against my body

i began to see shade
as normal
adjusting
to the night
to the cold
to being all alone

but one day
i saw you
sitting in the shade
shivering
and scared
waiting for the sun

i wasn't alone
but i wished it to be true
not that i didn't want

companionship
but
you
deserved so much more
than you could see
like
the sun
the moon
the stars

everything

so i promised to find the sun
for you

and in a moment
i'll never forget
you said
i light up your life

then i began to remember

i am the sun

and so

are you

-in the shade

shedding
light

i have lost sleep many times from anxiety
but tonight is different
i lost sleep because
i found one reason to remain awake

this book

in the shade is a collection of poetry that unfolds human struggle while empowering readers to view the world in a new lens. Shedding light on mental health, relationships, and self-discovery, *in the shade* intends to remove the darkness within.

Placed carefully into five chapters, *in the shade* signifies the healthy transition from rigid thinking to flexible thinking. Through each section, readers embark on a journey to gain a deeper understanding of the world.

in the shade reminds readers they have the ability to be the light in their own darkness and in the darkness of another.

-shedding light on the book

Dayna Gosselin is a self-published author born and raised in Sarnia, Ontario. In 2010, she pursued an Honors B.A in Criminology from Laurier University, then furthered her educational pursuit by obtaining her Social Service Worker Diploma from Fanshawe College.

Employed in the social service sector for two years, *Dayna Gosselin* has worked with individuals involved in the criminal justice system experiencing barriers within the community. While providing individualized support, she was inspired by these resilient individuals to write her poetry collection.

She hopes to inspire and empower individuals who may be struggling, to see that light can come from darkness.

Dayna Gosselin now resides in Whistler, British Columbia and continues to write, utilizing her poetry a therapeutic tool for self-discovery and healing.

-shedding light on the author

i hope you find inspiration in my words
like i have in all of you

9781775222606